T0322006

Elena:
A Hand Made Life

Elena:
A Hand Made Life

Miriam Gold

Jonathan Cape
London

Comforted years will sit soft-chaired,

In rooms of amber;

The years will stretch their hands, well-cheered

By our life's ember.

- From 'Miners', Wilfred Owen

1

My granny's hands yanked the gearstick of her red Austin Mini, grinding the gears as she charged around the streets of 1980s Leigh, Lancashire.

The sound of that crunch made you wince. Every two years she'd buy another secondhand Mini and burn out the gearbox. Remembering it now, I'm surprised she didn't have to replace them more often.

On visits to our granny and grandad, my brother Ben, being older, would sometimes get to sit in the front. Bendog, her standard poodle (named to differentiate from Benboy) snored and farted loudly on the back seat. I'd be squashed in next to him, green and silent with nausea, what with the dog's stink and her cornering.

In the Mini she'd do her rounds. Mornings were for the surgery, afternoons were for home visits. If I was staying she'd take me with her and I'd wait outside in the car with the windows wound down, gulping the fresh air. Occasionally, she'd take me into her patients' houses. Looking back, I'm surprised it was allowed. It probably wasn't.

'Come in Dr Zadik!' 'Hello dear! How's the family, where's the pain?' I would be given a biscuit, or if I was lucky, some sweets. Then, I would find a quiet corner to eat them, hoping no one would notice me.

But Granny would always point at me. 'That is my number one granddaughter visiting from London - not number one favourite, just the eldest!' she'd yell. She was quite deaf.

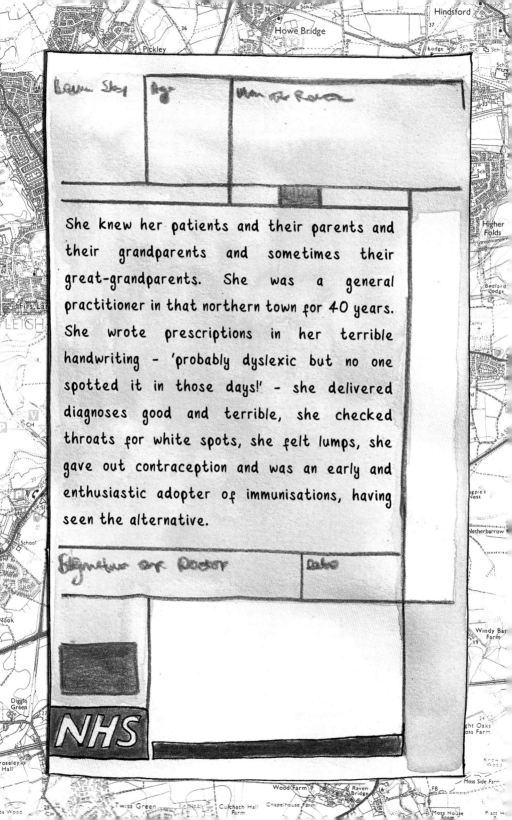

She knew her patients and their parents and their grandparents and sometimes their great-grandparents. She was a general practitioner in that northern town for 40 years. She wrote prescriptions in her terrible handwriting - 'probably dyslexic but no one spotted it in those days!' - she delivered diagnoses good and terrible, she checked throats for white spots, she felt lumps, she gave out contraception and was an early and enthusiastic adopter of immunisations, having seen the alternative.

She famously told it how it was, and she was a very well-respected doctor. She called a spade a bloody shovel did Dr Zadik, they said. She adored her busy work, not retiring until her 70th birthday and nearly the end of the century.

To walk around Leigh with her was to accompany a celebrity. Patients would stop her for a chat everywhere she went. A trip to the Post Office took most of the morning.

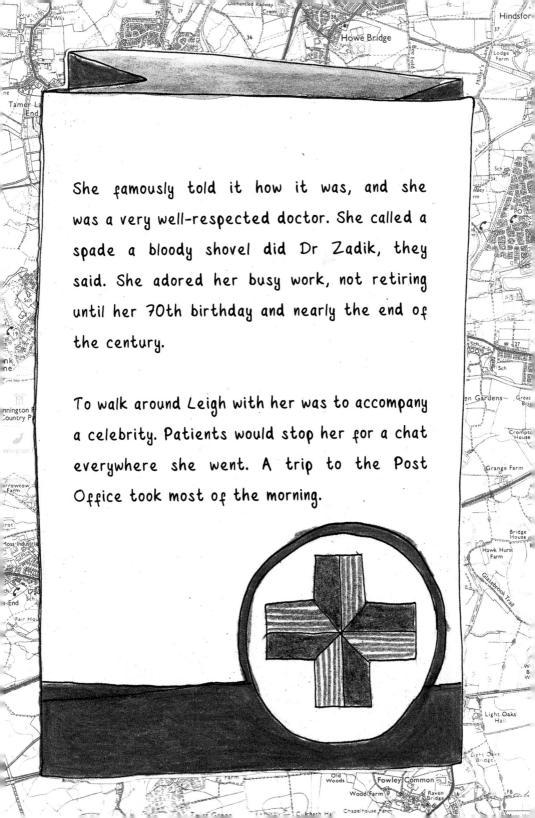

For a woman of medicine and science she was not very worldly. She told unintentionally filthy and hilarious stories about her work. Applying no filter to me, her young granddaughter, the facts of life were told plainly. We would walk, and she would talk.

'Did I ever tell you the one about the patient who came in saying, "Doctor, I'm expecting number 8, how could this have happened?" So I replied, "Well, didn't you use your cap like I showed you dear?" And so she said, (at this point Granny would already be giggling) "Oh yes, I sewed it up with my needle and thread so carefully after it tore!" '

Granny guffawed. Seeing my blank face, not getting the joke, she stopped laughing and said, 'Well, the point is dear, the hole was easily big enough for semen to pass through!'

Or the story – one of her very favourites – about the patient who owned a sweet shop and came to the surgery with what she thought was The Change, but Granny told her no, in fact she was pregnant and wished her congratulations. 'Eee! And it only happened once!' the woman said, 'and on the counter too!' Granny roared with laughter, and then stopped.

'The baby was stillborn, very sad,' she sniffed. 'Let's go home along the canal.'

Granny's hands gripped the steering wheel as though driving a bumper car, knuckles turning white and wrists bulging fleshily under her watchstrap.

'I've never taken a driving test!' she yelled, 'After the war, they just rushed us all through!' Hearing aid switched off and oblivious to the furious beeps from the other cars, she careered around the Lancashire roundabouts at least twice every time.

We'd quietly take over the wheel and do the bay parking for her in Manchester city centre. Staggering from the car, laughing and giddy with relief, crying:

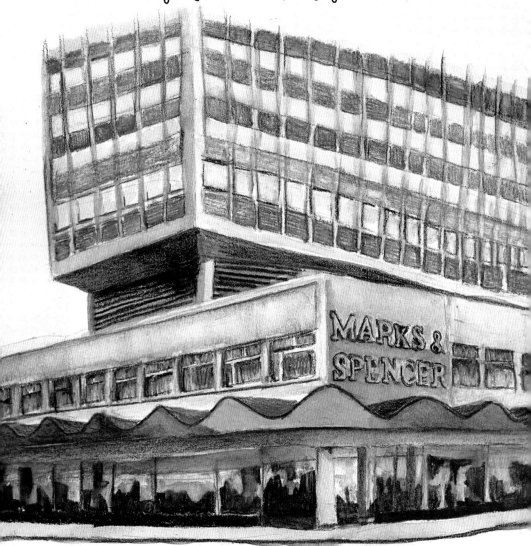

'We've made it! We're alive!' We'd kiss the pavement like the Pope. 'Oh bugger off you lot,' she'd mutter, 'I've never had a crash.' Into Manchester we'd go, legs still shaky from the drive, on the hunt for Chinese food and the big Marks for new knickers.

My granny's hands looked like this:

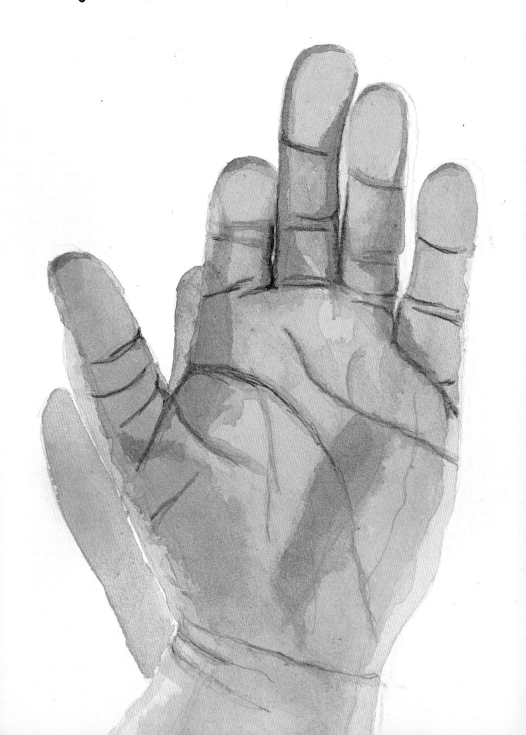

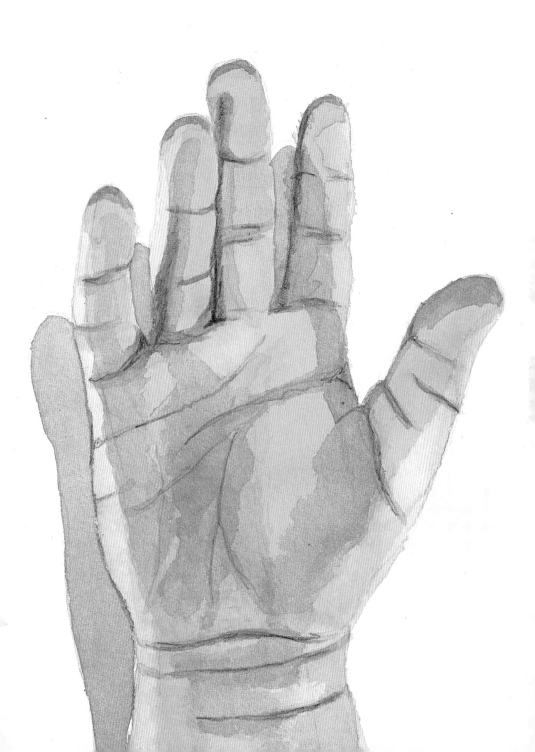

When she was 64

she slammed her hand

in her garage doors one

night — she was a prolific door slammer

— and the tip of her left index finger

came clean off. It was neatly sewn up

just below the joint.

My grandad told me he found the fingertip later that evening on the gravel by the neighbour's wall. I was horrified. 'What did you do with it?' I squeaked. 'Not much,' he said. 'I just sort of picked it up and dropped it.' Granny just said the accident improved her knitting.

It didn't stop those restless hands.

She wound the wool around her short finger, releasing the yarn and controlling the tension. A very efficient bobbin.

She knitted fast and she knitted tight, in the Continental style, not the lumbering British in-round-through-off.

Out of her hands would grow itchy hats and sweaters in a production line.

She had nine grandchildren to knit for. She would not do cartoon characters, and she would not do spaceships or fashionable colours.

Instead, skilled intarsia, cables, and ribs all thick, warm and sensible in browns and blues would emerge magically from her clacking needles and her crochet hook.

Granny slammed and crashed; Grandad quietly tidied it all up. He was a doctor too, an orthopaedic surgeon at Wigan Infirmary. In his spare time he painted, setting up an easel in the back bedroom for his oils and a mitre saw to make the frames. He was adored.

Every single evening Granny and Grandad went for a walk along the towpaths or in the woods beyond Lilford Park. On school holidays my cousins and I would stay with them, sleeping in strong cotton sheets washed soft and smooth.

We would get taken on their walks reluctantly, too scared of them to put up any serious resistance and secretly hoping the ice cream van would be parked outside the wrought-iron park gates.

They were busy. Knitting, crocheting, working, cooking, painting, gardening and boiling. My granny's hands picked fruit off the bushes in her garden and pulled an enormous aluminium pan down from the high shelf.

Jars boiled clean and neatly stacked on the shelves of her porch. She made jam every year, and every year complained it was too runny. Once, she found a jar of blackberry jam from 1979, by then at least a decade earlier.

She scraped off the mould and tucked in.

'It's only penicillin, for God's sake.'

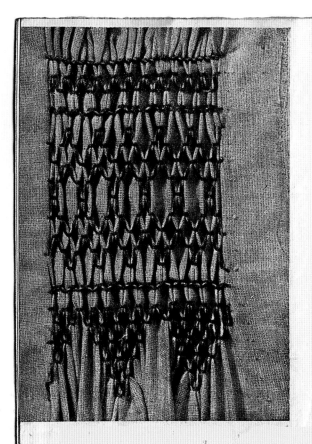

She smocked and sewed dresses for her daughters, and then much later for my cousins and me. Blues, browns, oranges and whites. Floral prints and polka dots. Never pink. If there was any fabric left over she'd make sturdy pairs of matching knickers.

FOR PANELS

PREPARE the gauging, then work a row of stem-stitches at the top line of gauging. Leave a space, then set in a row of surface honeycombing. Leave another space and work a row of cable-stitches (Diagrams I and 2).

Now work in surface honeycombing, forming it into the zig-zag pattern shown in Diagram 3. Leave a space after this is completed and work another row of cable-stitches.

Leave another space, then work in surface honeycombing, this time forming it into solid points. This stitch completes the pattern.

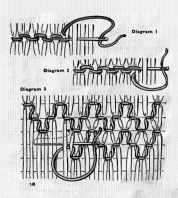

After the war she made them from parachute silk if she could not get cotton. I could not believe the skill, the tiny pleats and little geometric patterns: how did this magic happen? 'Well, you bought these sorts of bits of tracing paper,' she said, 'and that did the pattern for you.

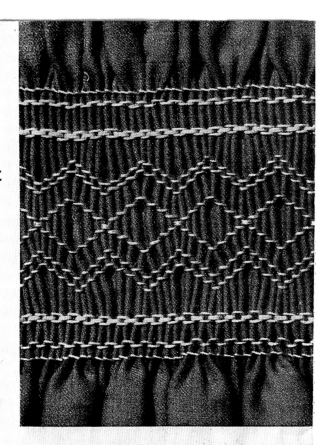

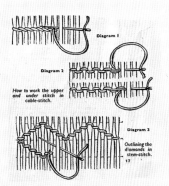

Diagram 1

Diagram 2

How to work the upper and under stitch in cable-stitch.

Diagram 3

Outlining the diamonds in stem-stitch.

17

Then, you made loose stitches and pulled the threads to gather it all together. It looks a lot more complicated than it actually is.'

DIAMOND POINTED

THIS pattern is worked in cable-stitch and surface honeycombing. Begin by making two rows of cable-stitch with the alternate stitches in each row touching. (Diagrams 1 and 2 show how cable-stitch is worked.)

Leave a short space, then commence the diamond pattern, which is worked entirely in surface honeycombing. Work a complete row of stitches in the first row, then begin and end the second row one stitch in. Begin the third row one stitch in from the row above, work seven stitches then fasten off. Work five stitches in the next row and complete the point with a row of three stitches. Form the second point in the same way.

The small diamond is set half-way between the two points a short distance down. Begin by working three honeycomb stitches, the top stitch in the centre. In the next two rows work five stitches and complete the diamond with a row of three stitches like the first row.

To work double cable-stitch begin the first row with the thread above the needle and travel from left to right. Pass over the first two pleats, then take a stitch through the top of the second pleat, pointing the needle from right to left (Diagram 1). Take a stitch through the second pleat, but with the thread below the needle (Diagram 2). Work another row of cable-stitch, but start with the thread below the needle for the first stitch, so that alternate stitches in the two rows come close together.

The honeycombing used in this pattern is worked from left to right. Bring the needle through from the back and oversew the first two pleats together, bringing the needle out between the pleats. Go down a little way, then oversew the second and third pleats together, inserting the needle between the pleats and bringing it out in the same place (Diagram 3). Go up again to the level of the first stitch made and sew the third and fourth pleats together in the same way (Diagram 4). Continue like this to the end of the work.

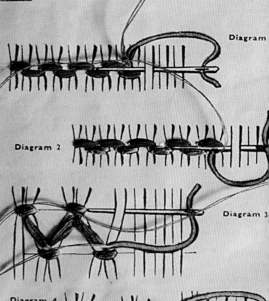

Diagram 1

Diagram 2

Diagram 3

Diagram 4

6

'We didn't get a
television until
1955 and you
couldn't get
clothes like you
do now so I just
made everything.

All women did.'

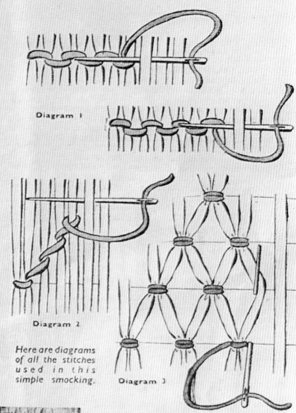

Diagram 1

Diagram 2

Here are diagrams
of all the stitches
used in this
simple smocking.   Diagram 3

Some of the little
dresses hang on
my wall now.
They are such
lovely things.

Gathering the threads together, all women did.
My granny's clever hands.

2

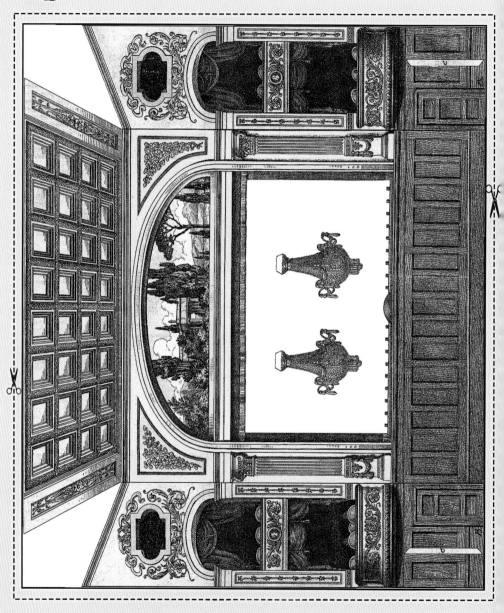

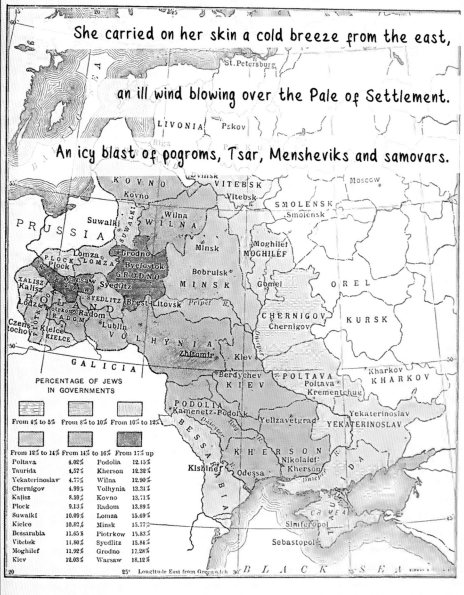

She carried on her skin a cold breeze from the east,

an ill wind blowing over the Pale of Settlement.

An icy blast of pogroms, Tsar, Mensheviks and samovars.

PERCENTAGE OF JEWS
IN GOVERNMENTS

From 4% to 5%   From 8% to 10%   From 10% to 12%

From 12% to 14% From 14% to 16% From 17% up

Poltava	4.02%	Podolia	12.15%
Taurida	4.57%	Kherson	12.32%
Yekaterinoslav	4.77%	Wilna	12.90%
Chernigov	4.99%	Volhynia	13.31%
Kalisz	8.59%	Kovno	13.71%
Plock	9.13%	Radom	13.89%
Suwalki	10.09%	Lomza	15.69%
Kielce	10.82%	Minsk	15.77%
Bessarabia	11.65%	Piotrkow	15.83%
Vitebsk	11.80%	Syedlitz	15.84%
Moghilef	11.92%	Grodno	17.28%
Kiev	12.03%	Warsaw	18.12%

MAP OF WESTERN RUSSIA SHOWING THE JEWISH PALE OF SETTLEMENT.

Granny's hands did not clap in
church on Sunday morning.

Thwacking a jar of rollmops on the side of the
kitchen worktop and yanking off the lid she said:

'I've been Lithuanian, Ukrainian, German and British. I've felt like a foreigner everywhere I've lived.

But I was born a Jew and I'll die a Jew.'

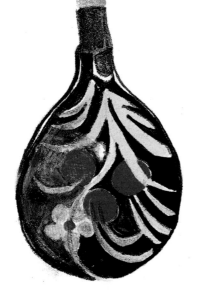

We ate our lunch. No more was said. Granny told me little of her early life, I collected crumbs and fragments.

Plates finished, a pause settled heavily over the tablecloth. 'And now? What will you eat?' My grandparents' faces turned to me anxiously, expectantly: 'What will you eat next? You've barely had any protein, you must eat more cheese.'

For nothing, nothing was worse than a thin child.

Elena Moisiegevna Mackeviciute, it said on her Lithuanian passport,

1924

was born in 1919 in Kharkiv, now in Ukraine.

She had two birthdays. Like the Queen.

The calendar was changed from Julian to Gregorian around the time of her birth.

So she could take her pick from 30 August or 12 September.

26

Her parents were Litvaks, from Vilnius. Her father, she claims, was so disappointed she wasn't a boy he ignored her for months.

It was during the Russian Civil War. He and his brother were imprisoned for having the wrong sort of politics. Menshevik and not Bolshevik.

Mother and baby
went to visit
him in prison
and through
the bars, she
smiled at him,
he at her.

And so began a
bond of mutual love,
understanding and
admiration only to
be broken by a
brutal and
untimely death.

Her parents were first cousins. It explains a lot, we giggled. Her grandmothers were sisters and did not approve of their children's match.

But, returning home from the theatre
in Moscow one night, one of the sisters
was killed by a ricocheting bullet. It was
the first night of Hanukkah 1918,
during the Russian Civil War. As she
lay dying, her hand was placed over the
entwined hands of the young lovers, so
as to bless their union. She died,
they were married.

As a child hearing this story from my mother,
I nearly exploded with questions:
a ricocheting bullet? Also: the dead hand!
Also: HER GRANDMOTHERS WERE *SISTERS!*
I always had more questions than answers.

СВОБОДА

СВОБОДА

СВ

Урядовий орган Українського Народного Союза — "SVOBODA" — Official organ of...

БОЛЬШЕВИКИ ПРОГНАЛИ ЛЯХІВ З КИЄВА

ПОЛЬСЬ

РЕСПУБЛІКАНСЬКА ПАРТІЯ НА КОНВЕНЦІЇ В ШІКАГО ... ДЖ. ГАРДІНГА. СЕН...

НА ДЕЛЕГАЦ

УКРАЇНСЬКІ ВІСТИ.

АМЕРИКА

МА КІНЦЯ ПОЛЬСЬКИМ ЗВІРСТВАМ В ГАЛИЧИ

ПОЛЬСЬКА ДЕЛЕГАЦІЯ В РИЗІ ВІДРІКЛАСЯ ПЕТЛЮРУ

УКРАЇНСЬКІ ВІСТИ.

АМЕРИКАНСЬКІ ВІСТИ.

З РІЖНИХ СТОРО

З ПОЛЬЩІ.

... товаришів У. С.-Д. Роб. Партії

Elena's mother's hands squeezed lemon juice all over her daughter's pale freckled skin. 'It will make the freckles fade,' she explained. But of course, it didn't. 'She'll never get a husband,' they all said, 'being so covered like that.' But of course, she did. And more besides. Her life took her far beyond Kharkiv and far from her mother's arms.

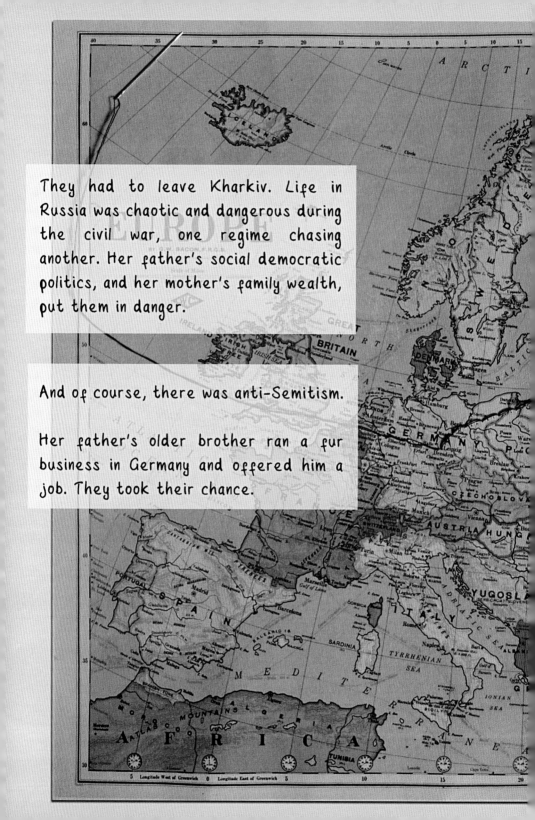

They had to leave Kharkiv. Life in Russia was chaotic and dangerous during the civil war, one regime chasing another. Her father's social democratic politics, and her mother's family wealth, put them in danger.

And of course, there was anti-Semitism.

Her father's older brother ran a fur business in Germany and offered him a job. They took their chance.

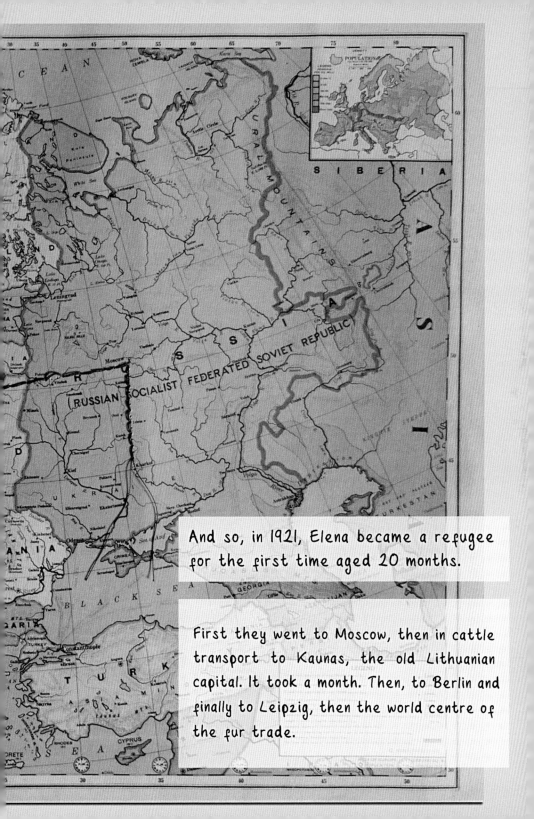

And so, in 1921, Elena became a refugee for the first time aged 20 months.

First they went to Moscow, then in cattle transport to Kaunas, the old Lithuanian capital. It took a month. Then, to Berlin and finally to Leipzig, then the world centre of the fur trade.

To Leipzig, then.

Elena was called an Osterjude, eastern Jew. Rough, and primitive and looked down upon by the German Jewish sophisticates. But Leipzig was a left-wing town of half a million immigrants and things could have been much worse for her family. She had something of a childhood and — for a good stretch — an education. When her school was inspected by the local Nazis, her teacher would warn her not to come in that day. In this way, she managed to stay in school.

In Leipzig, she saw something that changed her life. Elena lived with her parents in a room they shared with another family. A curtain divided the small space. Peeping out from behind it one day she saw a cupping treatment.

It fascinated her, what was this magic?

A spark was lit. Studying medicine, being a doctor, became all she wanted to do.

The spark never went out and carried her across countries and nationalities and a career that fascinated her for as long as she lived.

She told her parents her dream.

Her mama said, 'Why be a doctor when you can marry one?'

Her papa said, 'It's disgusting! You'll have to discuss people's bowels! You'll do all that study and then get married, have children and give it all up!'

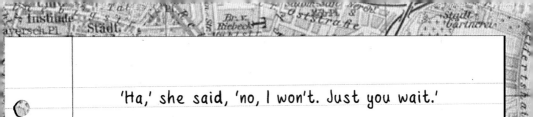

'Ha,' she said, 'no, I won't. Just you wait.'

By 1936 German doors were slamming shut
- or at least being kicked in - to Jews, no
chance of being a doctor now if she stayed.

Elena's uncle was the boss
of the family business.

He was terrible at it.

He was skilled with the furs but he ran up debts. 'Koif, koif: Gott werd zohlen,' he would say.

Buy, buy: God will pay.
But while he was getting around to paying, it fell to his younger brother, her papa, to underwrite him.

One morning they discovered her uncle, his wife and their son had left for Italy during the night. Her papa managed to arrange more loans from the bank to keep the business going. But it meant they could not leave.

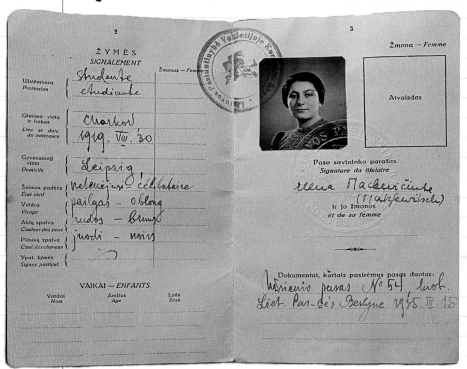

And so, her parents had to stay in Leipzig to pay off her uncle's debts.

The paying of the debts, it turned out,

cost them their lives.

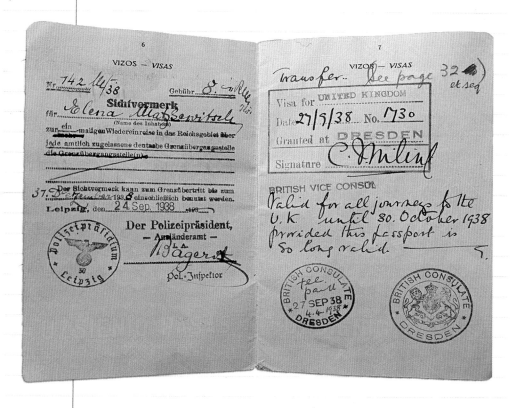

In April 1936, Elena left for England alone.

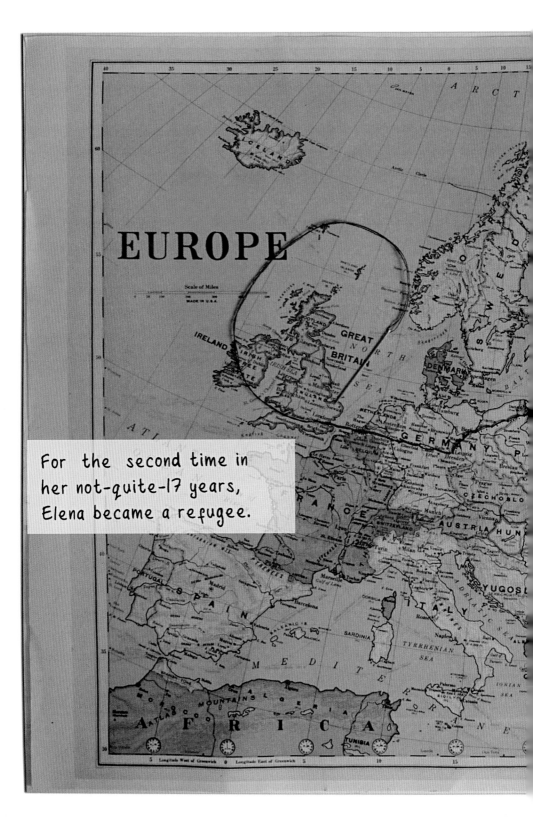

For the second time in her not-quite-17 years, Elena became a refugee.

Miss Matskevitch's hands — for
that was who she was now —
were covered in the most
awful chilblains. Although it
was April, London was freezing.
She boarded at a school for
German Jewish children in
Red Lion Square.

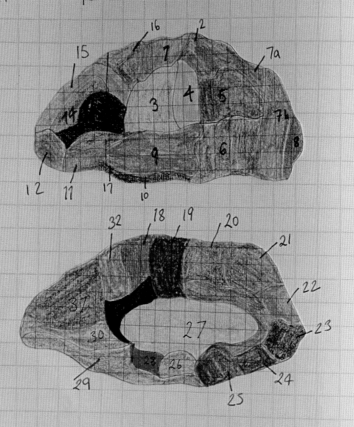

She continued her studies alone, determined to be a doctor. It was an act of blind faith, a defiance: who would want a female doctor? Without a British education? Or a proper address?

To get to medical school she needed the London Matriculation. But she only had until September. She crammed hard. English literature, English language, physics, mathematics.

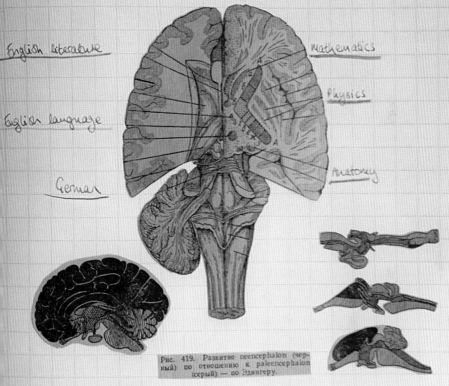

English literature

Mathematics

English language

Physics

German

Anatomy

Рис. 419. Развитие псеncephalon (черный) по отношению к paleencephalon (серый) — по Эдингеру.

She was the only one with this ambitious schedule, so the school put her to study by herself in a cold room in the basement.

Her mama was aghast at the timetable.

All her papa said was, 'She'll do it.'

Years later, by which time she was my granny, she told me she did not like London.

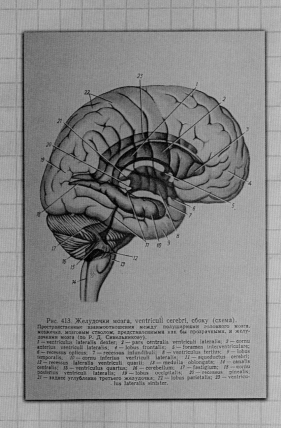

Рис. 413. Желудочки мозга, ventriculi cerebri, сбоку (схема).
Пространственные взаимоотношения между полушариями головного мозга, мозжечка, мозговым стволом, представленными как бы прозрачными, и желудочками мозга (по Р. Д. Синельникову).
1 — ventriculus lateralis dexter; 2 — pars centralis ventriculi lateralis; 3 — cornu anterius ventriculi lateralis; 4 — lobus frontalis; 5 — foramen interventriculare; 6 — recessus opticus; 7 — recessus infundibuli; 8 — ventriculus tertius; 9 — lobus temporalis; 10 — cornu inferius ventriculi lateralis; 11 — aqueductus cerebri; 12 — recessus lateralis ventriculi quarti; 13 — medulla oblongata; 14 — canalis centralis; 15 — ventriculus quartus; 16 — cerebellum; 17 — fastigium; 18 — cornu posterius ventriculi lateralis; 19 — lobus occipitalis; 20 — recessus pinealis; 21 — заднее углубление третьего желудочка; 22 — lobus parietalis; 23 — ventriculus lateralis sinister.

But I was a London native, the city was my playground. How could you not like London? Now, thinking of her, little more than a child, alone in a cold dark basement, separated from her family and not allowed to study with the other students. Well.

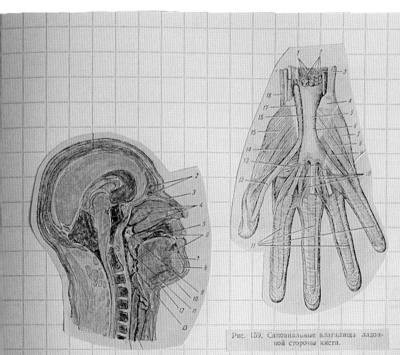

Рис. 159. Синовиальные влагалища ладонной стороны кисти.

She did it. Of course she did. She passed in the highest group and got a place at Sheffield Medical School. She wrote to her parents and told them the good news.

And so, Miss Matskevitsch became the other thing she always was: a Northerner.

N

At Sheffield station Elena's
hands clutched the handle of her suitcase.

The air was so filthy she could see it.

She nearly turned back.

Back to where though?

News of her arrival reached the

Jews of Sheffield. They mobilised.

They took her in and found her

lodgings with a family near the

medical school. But after a year,

her parents could no longer

afford to send her money.

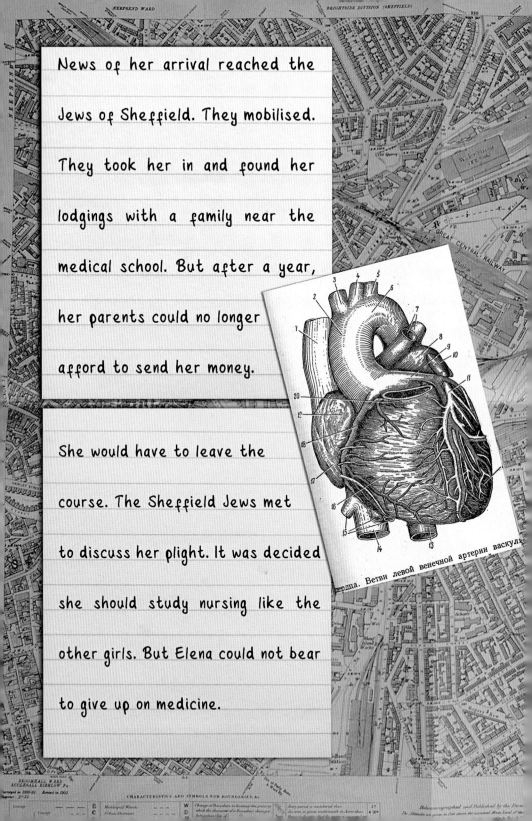

Ветви левой венечной артерии васкул

She would have to leave the

course. The Sheffield Jews met

to discuss her plight. It was decided

she should study nursing like the

other girls. But Elena could not bear

to give up on medicine.

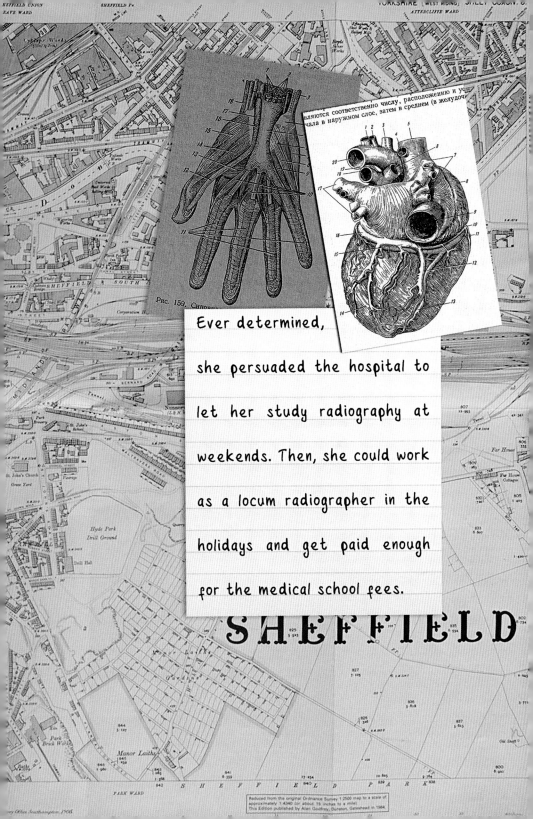

Ever determined, she persuaded the hospital to let her study radiography at weekends. Then, she could work as a locum radiographer in the holidays and get paid enough for the medical school fees.

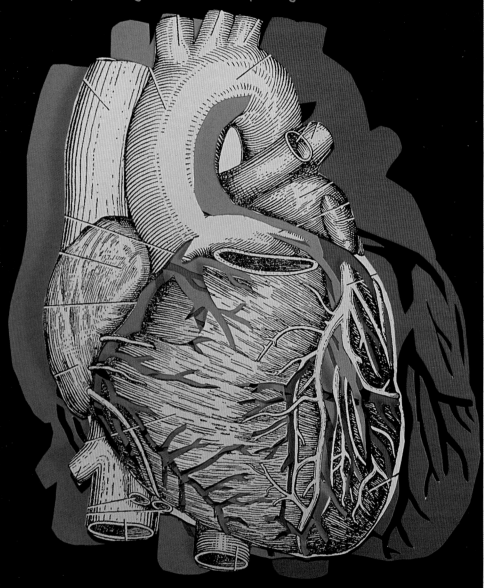

A fourth-year medic, five years her senior

and a German Jew, kept appearing.
There was common ground between them,

a shared language for things that were unspeakable.

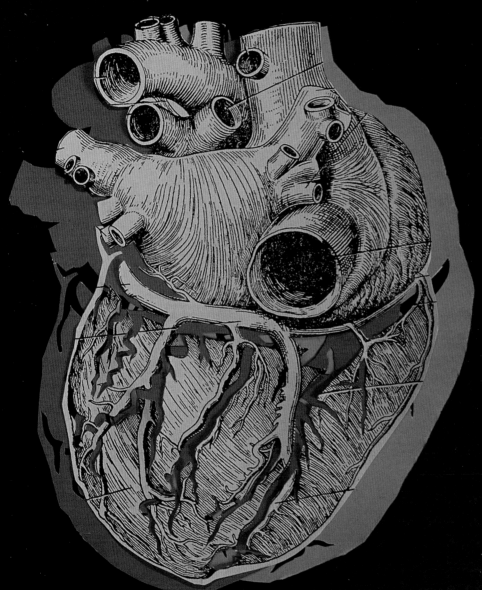

He too was a refugee, from Hamburg, and
all alone in the cold country.

He began to write her poetry.

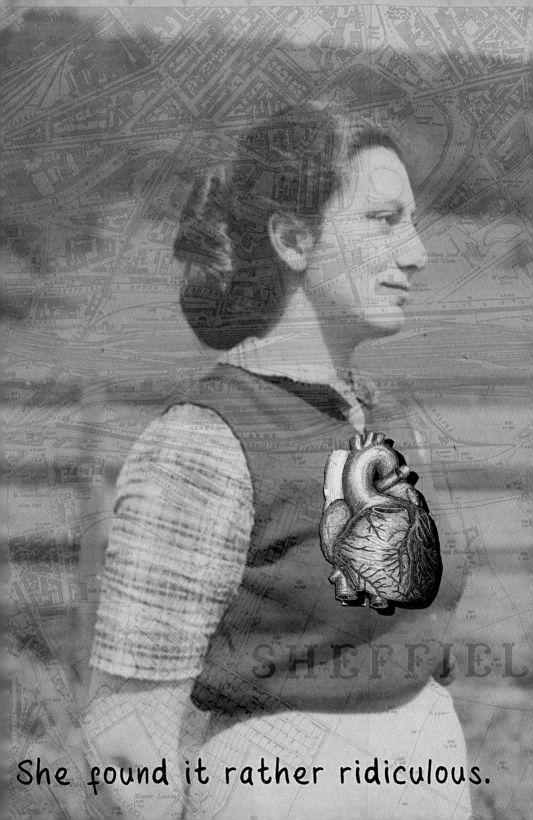

She found it rather ridiculous.

But they both loved hiking and the Peak District was there to explore, so off they went.

They pooled their meagre finances to split a twopenny ice instead of catching the tram home.

Stanage Edge, Rivelin Dams,
Hathersage; a few short
years after the Kinder
Scout mass trespass,
they walked and talked the length and breadth
of the Peak District. Stateless both of them,
that land was their land.

She was Lena to him.

He, Franz to her. Frank to the medical school. His persistence won out; by 1939 they were engaged. But the rules were the rules: no married resident staff at the hospital where he was a junior surgeon. His job was also his home, and he could not afford to lose either. Synagogue booked, cake baked, the wedding had to be cancelled at the last minute.

compared to what was coming.

VIA AIR MAIL

PASSED BY CENSOR 49.

4

In 1940 the British government was panicked and febrile. The talk was of fifth-columnists and espionage. Franz Zadik was both German - and therefore an 'enemy alien' - and a Jewish refugee. He had been summoned to a tribunal and classified as a 'friendly alien'. But was it enough?

No. He lost his job and his accommodation. He was arrested and sent to Canada to an internment camp, and then to another on the Isle of Man.

Elena's landlady said she couldn't house the fiancée of an enemy of the people and she was made homeless too. She went back to the Jewish family near the hospital who had been so kind to her.

Through it all, she knitted generously and abundantly. Frank, his brother and fellow internees received warm sweaters, hats, gloves to keep out the Canadian cold.

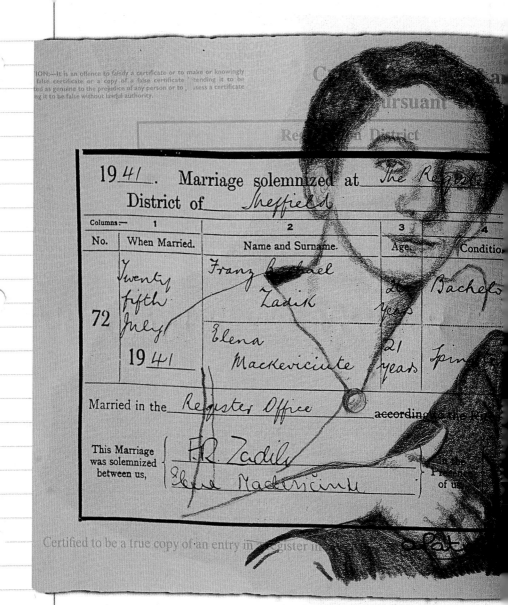

1941. Marriage solemnized at _The Regis..._
District of _Sheffield_

No.	When Married.	Name and Surname.	Age.	Conditio...
72	Twenty fifth July 1941	Franz Michael Zadik	2... years	Bachelo...
		Elena Mackeviciute	21 years	Spin...

Married in the _Register Office_ according to the R...

This Marriage was solemnized between us, — F.R. Zadik — Elena Mackeviciute — ...in the Presence of us...

By 1941 the panic subsided; the British policy of interning German Jews wound down. Frank wrote that if he had a job, he could be released. Elena pleaded at the hospital for him to get his old job back. But the head of staff said there was nothing he could do.

AA248023

M. Cert.

S.R./R.B.D

...rriage Act

...FIELD

in the

County Borough of Sheffield

5	6	. 7	8
or Profession.	Residence at the time of marriage.	Father's Name and Surname.	Rank or Profession of Father.
...ical ...ctitioner	_Royal Hospital Sheffield_	_Manfred Zadik_	_Solicitor_
	...ndcliffe ... Sheffield	_...ejus ...kevicius_	_Farmer_
		by _Certificate before_ by me, _J. M. Kearney._	
		Deputy Registrar	
		C Barber	
		Supt. Registrar	

Registrar   Date

Her kind radiographer boss, the same man who
had given her a job to pay her fees and stay at
the medical school, found her sobbing. Mr Grout
was his name. He said he'd see what he could do.
Ten minutes later he returned and said Frank
had a job. And so, Frank was finally released. He
came home, they were married.

We must not forget the Boutonnieres for the gentlemen. Correctness demands that nothing be omitted.

Elena's hands wore a wire-thin wedding ring. She wanted 22 carat gold but had only 2 guineas. They raised just enough for a taxi to the registry office.

She made her own dress and floral spray, not the bouquet she really wanted. A tea at Cole Brothers for 12 marked the start of their 57 years of marriage.

By marrying Frank she became a German citizen and so also classed as an enemy alien, though of course she was the enemy of the enemy. Even though, as a Jew, Frank had been stripped of his German citizenship. It was labyrinthine.

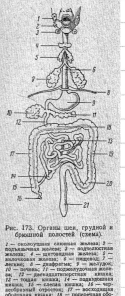

Into the maze went freedom of movement. In order to leave Sheffield for a honeymoon she had to use her

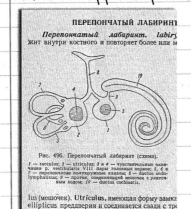

maiden name to hide their German citizenship. But where could they stay? In those days, unmarried couples could not share a room. Elena wrote to her MP for help and with her intervention, the newlyweds spent three days in Hathersage.

Eleanor Rathbone was their MP; she'd also campaigned for an end to the internment of 'enemy aliens'. In 1937 she'd organised the rescue of 4,000 children from the Basque combat zone during the Spanish Civil War. In 1942 she spoke in the houses of Parliament, calling on the government and the BBC to publicise evidence of the Holocaust.

It is also thanks to Eleanor Rathbone - a Liverpudlian and a suffragette - that we have family allowance.

Oh Eleanor Rathbone.

Years later, a student at Liverpool University, I went most days to the Eleanor Rathbone Building. I signed many petitions, I went on marches. In the canteen by the entrance, I drank a lot of tea. But I did not start family allowance, I did not organise boats that got around a blockade, and I did not have any idea of her direct involvement in my family's story.

If peace came tomorrow, we could not forget the millions for whom it would come too late, nor wash our hands of the stain of blood - Eleanor Rathbone

Caught in the crosshairs of institutional sexism, racism and internment, as enemy aliens and refugees, Elena and Frank's lives and choices were bound by intrusion. There was no privacy. They could not live as man and wife if they wanted jobs in hospitals.

And Elena could not be pregnant. She was shamed and told to wear discreet clothing to hide the sure signs. At her student exam in public health and forensic medicine the external examiner took one look at her and asked her to list the causes of maternal mortality.

Mrs Zadik - as she was now and delighted to have only 5 letters to spell - had such incredibly busy hands. Knitting and crocheting clothes for her baby under the desks during her lectures, taking her finals when he was just 6 months old.

She graduated before his first birthday.

They adjusted her exams to fit

around his feeds. By this point in the

war the hospitals were so short-staffed

they had to employ married doctors, even

female ones.

And so she got her first job.

A doctor at last.

At this time, she and her baby were quite alone. Franz Zadik had become the safer, less Jewish-sounding Frank Young, and a doctor in the British Army, first in India, then West Africa, then Burma. During leave, a second baby, my mother, was made. Father and daughter would not meet until 1946 when he finally came home.

There was no maternity leave. No parents or family to help. No one to do the night feeds, or any feeds at all. She paid for help while she worked. She was barely 25.

Elena worked
so hard.

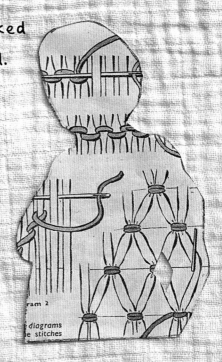

ram 2

e diagrams
e stitches

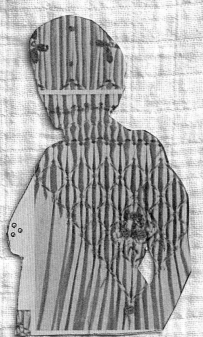

e small diamon
en the two points
wn. Begin by workin
mb stitches, the top stitch
the next two rows work
complete the diamond w
e stitches like the first
work double cable-stit
row with the threa
and travel from
er the first two pl
hrough the top
ting the needle
am 1). Take a stitch t
nd pleat, but with the t
the needle (Diagram 2). W
er row of cable-stitch, but st
the thread below the needle t
first stitch, so that alternate stitche
the two rows come close together.
The honeycombing used in this pattern
is worked from left to right. Bring the
needle through from the back and oversew the first two pleats together, bringing the needle out between the pleats.
Go down a little way, then oversew the
second and third pleats together, inserting the needle between the pleats and
bringing it out in the same place
(Diagram 3). Go up again to the level of
the first stitch made and sew the third
and fourth pleats together in the same
way (Diagram 4). Continue like this to
the end of the work.

Morning surgeries, evening surgeries, moving house,
delivering babies, a night fire warden. Such a young woman.

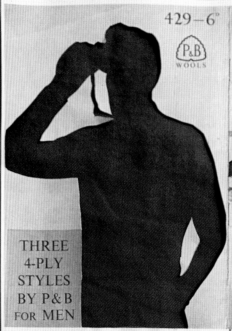

THREE
4-PLY
STYLES
BY P&B
FOR MEN

429—6ᵈ

P&B WOOLS

THREE
4-PLY
STYLES
BY P&B
FOR MEN

THREE 4-PLY STYLES FOR MEN

Please read this first

ABBREVIATIONS

K.=Knit; P.=Purl; K.B.=knit into back of stitch; P.B.=purl into back of stitch; st.=stitch; tog.=together; t.b.l. =through back of loops; inc.=increase by working into front and back of stitch; dec.=decrease by working 2 sts. together; beg.=beginning; alt.=alternate; rep.=repeat; patt.=pattern; incl. =inclusive; ⬩⬩⬩⬩ M.1.=Make 1 by p⬩⬩⬩⬩⬩⬩⬩⬩ lies between st. ⬩⬩⬩⬩⬩⬩⬩⬩⬩⬩ g st. and kni⬩⬩⬩⬩⬩⬩⬩⬩⬩ Cable 2 Front ⬩⬩⬩⬩⬩⬩⬩ sts. as follows⬩⬩⬩⬩⬩⬩⬩⬩ cable needle a⬩⬩⬩⬩⬩⬩⬩ rk, knit next 2 st⬩⬩⬩⬩⬩⬩ from cable needle; C2B⬩⬩⬩⬩⬩⬩ but leave sts. ⬩⬩⬩⬩⬩⬩ front; C⬩⬩⬩⬩⬩⬩⬩ next 8 ⬩⬩⬩⬩⬩⬩ on to⬩⬩⬩⬩⬩ work⬩⬩⬩⬩⬩ fro⬩⬩⬩⬩ line⬩⬩⬩ wit⬩⬩⬩

needles and some Patons Beehive Fingering 4-ply, Patonised, or Patons Purple Heather Fingering 4-ply. Cast on 14 stitches and work in stocking stitch— 1 row knit; 1 row purl—for 18 rows. Cast off; press lightly on wrong side. The tension should be 7 stitches and 9 rows to one square inch and the knitted square should measure 2 inches each way. If the square is bigger your work is too loose; try a size finer needle. If it is smaller your work is too tight; try a size coarser needle.
If you knit to the correct tension in stocking stitch, you will knit naturally to the correct tension for any stitch in this booklet. If you alter the needles to ⬩⬩⬩⬩⬩⬩⬩⬩ion in stocking ⬩⬩⬩⬩⬩⬩⬩lterations must ⬩⬩⬩⬩⬩⬩ throughout.
⬩⬩⬩⬩e round brackets ⬩⬩⬩⬩umber of times ⬩⬩⬩⬩ brackets, and all ⬩⬩⬩⬩ brackets to be ⬩⬩⬩⬩e of times stated ⬩⬩⬩kets.

⬩⬩⬩ES
⬩⬩⬩re brackets [ ] refer ⬩⬩⬩ large sizes respec-

⬩⬩⬩IRIES
⬩⬩⬩tting enquiries con-⬩⬩⬩klet to Dept. SHB, ⬩⬩⬩s Limited, Great West ⬩⬩⬩ Middlesex.

⬩⬩⬩r start on page 4

429

She knitted and knitted. It was a
compulsion. Balaclava helmets, socks,
scarves, pairs of gloves for the soldiers
all wrapped up in parcels and sent far away.
Did they ever get there? She could
never be sure.

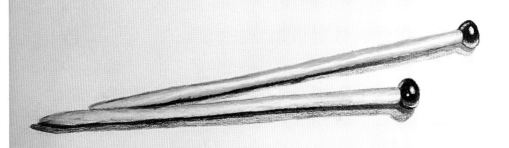

Meanwhile, the letters from her parents
had become Red Cross telegrams.
And then they stopped.

She was lonely, depressed and overwhelmed.

On the Luftwaffe flight path to Liverpool, Sheffield had a vicious blitz. Ten hours overnight in the air raid shelter was common. The planes would drop leftover bombs on the city on their way home from attacking the docks on the Mersey. Back-to-back houses and shared privies, the heavy industry and the mining provided little work for the women left behind.

The pay their husbands sent back was not enough. The British Army was class-ridden, and their men were privates. The air was so dirty the baby's pram sheets needed changing 3 times a day. Penistone Road, Langsett Road, 5 storeys high and a family in each room, and always water running down the walls.

The grim poverty of wartime Sheffield. Elena saw things you read about in history books: rheumatic fever, diphtheria, poliomyelitis; she went to a family of 8 where all the children died, one after the other, of tuberculous meningitis.

People were old at 60, and rarely saw 70. Doctors had to be paid, medicine bought. Even if it was life-saving, it was too expensive.

Dr Zadik's hands twitched helplessly. She was desperate to do follow-up visits for free if there was a sick child, but she was not allowed. It was miserable. She couldn't do it in secret as her boss knew all her visits and counted her money.

She longed for a comprehensive health service.

The war years ground on. What of her parents?

It turned out, Sonia and Moisie witnessed Kristallnacht. They were part of a secret network helping to hide other Jews. They had to leave Leipzig urgently. They fled to a village near Grasse in the South of France and lived quietly on a smallholding. They raised chickens and kept bees and found it rather suited them.

Through letters, they learned of Elena's qualification, her marriage and her baby. They were supportive and caring.

LL 1. GRASSE — Vue générale

A stack of letters from this briefly peaceful time survives in a cigar box. They are full of quotidian parental love, and are utterly devastating.

Daughter dear. How are your studies? When do you sit your exams? Are you comfortable? Is it very cold? Do you have enough money? We'll try and send something. Don't worry about us, we are fine.

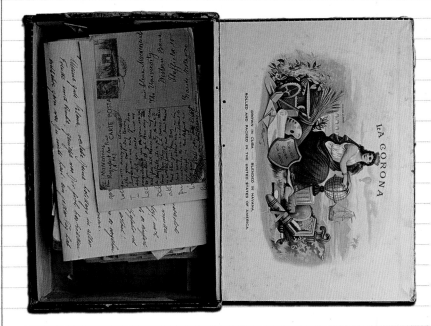

The letters become Red Cross telegrams. And then, they stop. Elena had no news for over three years. As the news about the camps emerged after the Allied liberation, she feared the worst.

CABLE AND WIRELESS

"Via Imperial"

391

22 FEB/94

ROQUEFORT LES PINS
= ELT MACKEVICIUTE UNIVERSITY SHEFFIELD =
DAUGHTER DARLING THANK TELEGRAM EVRY
WRITTING VIA PORTUAL AIR MAIL EVERYTHING
ALRIGHT LOVE FRANZ FINESTONES BONDY KISSING
BLESSING SUCCESS EAXINNATION .
MACKVICIUS .

Vichy France fell in 1942. A White Russian, somehow connected to their farm, denounced them to the Gestapo. Their cousin Eva had moved to the village with them and was out on an errand at the time of the arrest. Some of the villagers, who had seen their capture, warned Eva not to return to her house and hid her in the woods for 10 days.

The arrest happened some time in early 1944.
They were deported north, to the Parisian suburb
of Drancy and the transit camp.

An eyewitness confirmed their fate.

From Vilnius to Kharkiv to Leipzig to Grasse to
Drancy to Auschwitz.

5

How did she manage?

All those endless impossible

exhausting days. When I became a

mother, some days getting out

the front door with the children

in clean clothes nearly broke me.

How did she

To do:
- call clinic
- milk
  bread
  sausages
- edit PowerPoint
- Call James back
- SAFEGUARDING MEETING 2pm
- Sort out ParentPay → DINNERS
- Get clay   → MAKE EXEMPLARS FOR Y8
- N → socks
- Tell mum about Thursday

WATCH THE FIRES IN THE SKY AT NIGHT

GET TO WORK ON TIME

SEE HER PATIENTS ALL DAY

Change the sheets   Make the clothes

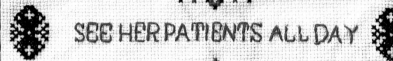

HOLD IT ALL TOGETHER

EAT THE MEALS TO MAKE THE MILK
TO FEED THE BABY

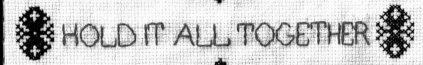

ALL WITH HER DEAD PARENTS AND
HER FAR-AWAY HUSBAND

In Elena's Northern city, built from steel, there was no talk of diaspora, or survivor's guilt, no words for PTSD. No language for postpartum depression or the agonising loneliness of a new mother.

No one spoke of trauma.

They had all just fought a war.

They were exhausted.

She finally learned of her parents' deaths in these years after the war ended: the survivors returned from the camps and her parents were not among them. Her cousin travelled to Sheffield from the village in France to tell her in person.

To a young female immigrant Jewish doctor, the glass ceiling, institutional sexism and systemic racism had not yet been invented.

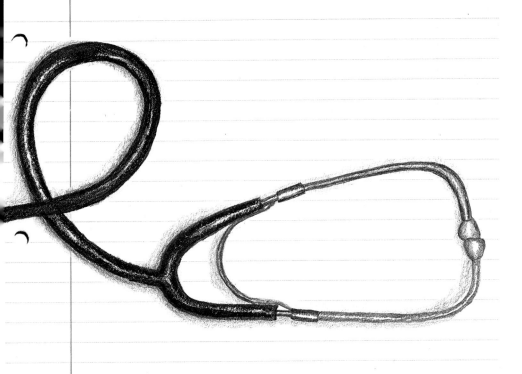

They were just how it was.

And so,
she just kept on.
One foot in front of
the other, sink or swim.

She swam.

And swam,

and swam.

She said the founding of the National Health Service in 1948 was the best day of her life. Even better than the births of her own children.

For, she said, her babies' births were a joy for her and Grandad, but the health service was a joy for everyone. Thinking of that family of 8 children dying one after the other, well.

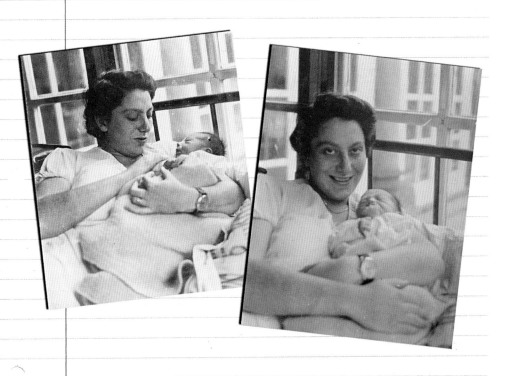

My granny's busy, wonderful hands.

She told me this often — by then she had the older person's habit of repeating herself — and I listened as I held my Granny's hand as we walked along the canal towpath.

By this time it was the 1980s and her NHS was under attack; in fact, an entire Lancastrian way of life was under attack.

In 1950 new jobs took them over the Pennines to Leigh, Lancashire, and a new life and a fourth baby.

My grandfather got a job at Wigan Infirmary, working with the surgeon who pioneered joint replacements.

Along the Bridgewater Canal we walked, over the new hills and parks laid out after the collieries had gone. Through the long grass growing over what was once a slag heap. Huge pitheads erased from the landscape. Scars left by devastating cuts. Granny's hands gripped her walking stick as she told me her stories.

'Everyone here had a job in the pits, mills or factories,' she said. The street names bore it out: Mill Street, Foundry Street and Spinning Jenny Way. 'When we moved here they made the underwear for Marks and Spencer. All my patients worked in the factories or the mines.

'People here had no education in those days and they had big families. There was enough work for everyone. Those two-up-two-down houses were like palaces when you went inside. People kept them so nicely. You'd see the pit ponies trotting down the street. The pit brow girls wearing shawls and clogs would clatter past. The sound soothed us to sleep. It was a busy place.

'We'd get woken up by the siren sounding the shift change at the pit. I would chase after the pit pony, shovelling up manure for the roses.'

To my young Southern ears it sounded like another world, a ghost story. Granny and Grandad had a poster of a Bruegel painting in their back bedroom, where I sometimes slept. Teeming with life and people working. I thought this must be what Leigh used to look like.

Dr Zadik's hands signed the papers for the opening of the Grasmere Street Surgery. A purpose-built, entirely modern health centre to serve the people of Leigh, housing GPs, health visitors, a pharmacy, welfare clinics and district nurses. For the last 15 years of her working life she went to work happy every single day in that team. An only child from a small decimated family, always feeling like an outsider, she had a strong sense of belonging among the receptionists, patients and fellow doctors.

Welcome to

We grandchildren would be taken in to visit her in the surgery to be cooed over by the women on reception. They would give us a pen and a prescription pad to draw on if we got bored. They all seemed to have a perm and set and a stout bosom. They regarded Granny with a mix of pride, fear and admiration. Even as children, we could sense it.

Grasmere St Surgery

She didn't retire until she was 70. 'What will she do with herself when she finally stops?' everyone asked.

What will she *DO*?

Granny applied the same aesthetic philosophy to her ceramics as she did her knitting: it must be sensible, useful

and BROWN!

She took up pottery, going to CLASSES at the

LOCAL ADULT EDUCATION CENTRE

She installed a potter's wheel in her shed. Her strong hands gripped the clay, forcing out the forms. A brisk production line of leaky teapots and pot after sensible brown pot.

She found plenty to do, of course. As well as all the brown pots there were letters to be written to her MP, lunchtime concerts to go to, walks to take, birds to watch and photographs to take. She could not bear to be still.

She had always taken photographs and in retirement filled album after album. Carefully labelled, they show her life in all its stages. Children, grandchildren, travels and walks, all seen through her lens.

I especially loved the ones she took on her walks around Leigh, everyday life eternally in black and white.

Fish and chip shops, flowers and canal boats. Granny's Leigh photos capture a vanished way of life. The huge wheel that drove the lift shaft, plunging the miners more than a mile underground, is now gone from the landscape.

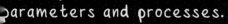

We were used to seeing her with a camera around her neck. Photography suited her. Visual, methodical and productive - much like knitting. Granny's creativity creativity flourished within parameters and processes.

She would struggle to express herself, growing angry and frustrated reaching for words she could not grasp. She had learned to speak, read and write in several languages with different scripts. And, she was dyslexic. Perhaps photography allowed her to communicate without such troublesome demands.

She printed her photographs herself. They are covered in marks where she did not rinse the chemicals off properly. She was not a great one for finesse. Or patience, her prints underdeveloped as she never let them expose long enough.

For my 8th birthday she bought me a little Russian camera, at 13 a photographic enlarger. I went to stay and she taught me how to print. Granny's strong hands heaved wooden blackout boards over the windows of her bathroom and changed the lightbulb to red.

Next, she hung a piece of string over the bath to peg the prints out to dry. She showed me how to tilt the tray of developing fluid, coaxing out the image on the paper. I loved the salty chemical smell and the rhythm of

develop   stop   fix

My camera, all snug inside its own carry case, was magic. I loved all the little jobs you had to do: press the exposure lever down until it clicked, wind on the film and catch the holes on the sprockets.

At weekends my grandparents would go for long walks in the hills of North Wales, a place they loved very much.

Granny's photographs from there show quizzical sheep standing in a row, and gnarled trees growing at right angles, bent by the wind over the mountains.

She bought an early digital camcorder and it accompanied her everywhere for a few years in a comically huge briefcase. My cousins and I were wearily resigned to being her models.

Filming, photographing, potting, painting and walking, the tempo of their busy retirement slowed as my grandfather grew ill, his kidneys failing him.

The trips to North Wales eventually stopped. After his death she said she couldn't bear to go.

This is not to say she was easy. Of course she was not easy. She was complicated. She was tough and she could be mean.

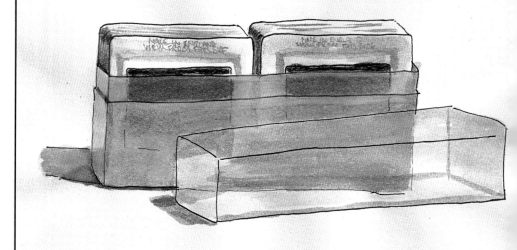

She would explode with rage and her children suffered her bad temper; being her grandchild was far easier.

She was known for her public stand-up rows.
She called herself She Who Must Be Obeyed.
And was not really joking. She was stridently
and volubly opinionated.

She was not reflective, and she wasn't much
for feelings, but then again, what good would
feelings have done her?

She grew more badly behaved with age.

My granny's hands gripped her cane tightly as she tapped the plinths in the art gallery. Looking around her, in the loud tones of the slightly deaf she yelled, 'Call this stuff *art*?' *Tap-tap* went her cane, terrifyingly close to the sculptures. 'And this?' *Tap-tap*. 'I mean, *what is it*?'

I kept a special apologetic smile for gallery assistants, shopkeepers, petrol station managers and anyone else I encountered on a day out with Granny. She thoroughly enjoyed the privilege of being old and naughty.

In the aisles of Asda, looking at the dates on the prawn sandwiches, she'd yell, 'Just look at the size of that woman's legs!' Bold as you please. We'd eat our sandwiches on a bench by the lake at Pennington Flash, throwing our crusts to the birds.

She looked into the water, remembering. 'You never saw fat people round here,' she said. I winced silently. 'Everyone worked too hard to be fat. Now look. Everyone eats in the street. Just walking along and stuffing their faces. The jobs all went then people got fat.'

It was my great fortune to know her into my adulthood. We had our days out and our walks, and we had our routine down: she told me her stories on repeat and I listened as though I had never heard them before, all catered by the sandwiches, and carrot cake from Greenhalgh's.

She had half-round glasses on a cord around her neck and wisps of grey hair escaping her bun. She spoke very little about the past, never about her childhood or the war years. This was not uncommon.

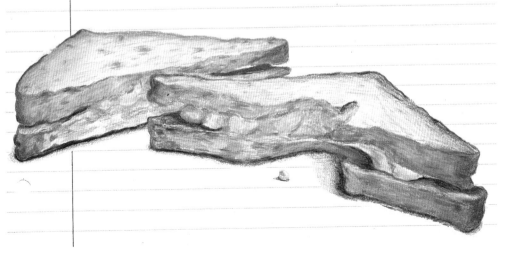

My memories of Granny's house are warm, safe and brown. Weak tea from a Denby mug. A brown-and-orange flowery plastic tray. Vintage before there was such a thing. Brown rugs in the lounge and brown cushions on the brown synthetic velvet sofa. On her Hornsea plates were two sensible solid brown stripes. Not beautiful but functional. A quality she prized higher than beauty.

Granny's neat house smelled of fabric conditioner. She always had sheets hanging on the wooden pulley clothes rack fixed to the kitchen ceiling. Drying against the immersion heater and wafting a warm sweet chemical smell around the house.

Granny's hands shook as she fumbled with the partitions in her pill box. This one for water driving, this one for cholesterol, this one for blood pressure. She went pale and floppy after lunch, head in hands.

She slumped against the radiator in the kitchen. I quietly made the tea and cleared away the lunch things, willing the colour back to her cheeks.

She had been a widow for a decade by this time. Old age was an arduous task, I saw this with every visit. Lancastrian winter nights began early: by half past three it was dark and the front door was bolted. It was a lonely marathon and you needed reserves of strength.

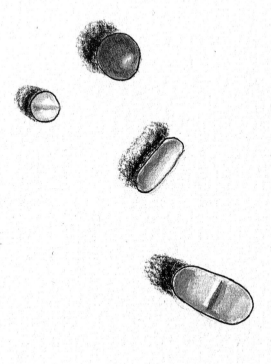

She had an enormous dark brown sideboard. The third drawer was full of chocolate, all slightly out of date. Tubes and bags of whiteish chocolate.

The sweet cocoa brown of the chocolate drawer. If I close my eyes I can capture, for a moment, the smell of stale chocolate and teak.

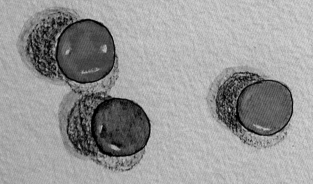

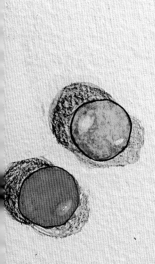
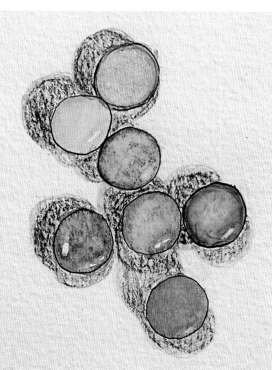

But go a little way beyond the hum of the immersion heater, open a cupboard door, and there were terrible things.

One day, in her 82nd year, at the start of a new millennium, my granny's hands were gripping her mug of tea. Matchstick men printed onto bone china. Proper art. She took her tea weak and black. 'Gnat's piss, my patients used to call it!' she snorted with delight, hunching over the steam.

She liked to watch Countdown while she had her tea and it had just finished. I remember the table was covered in scrunched-up pieces of paper where she'd tried to get the conundrum.

Then out of the blue she said,

'Do you know, if I met the people that killed my parents, I wouldn't want to do them harm. I mean, if they were lying in the gutter, if they were hurting on the side of the street I'd help them up, I wouldn't kick them back down. I don't bear grudges.'

A door had been flung
open to the past and
now the kitchen was
full of death.

I thought about what she'd said, and that I probably did. Bear grudges.

When I was a child I lived, as children do, half in my head and half in the world. I tried to understand the terrible things as best I could. I was told my history young, and plainly, and the brutal facts occupied strange liminal spaces at the edges of my thoughts. A kindly uncle with sweets in his pockets would visit from Canada and my parents' voices would lower: 'He was one of the last 3 alive when they opened the cattle trucks at Mauthausen.' It was so much. That nice man? In his dandy suit and pocket hankerchief?

How could such a thing even be real?

For Granny's was not the only history I inherited.

There were many others. My lovely, warm-hearted

great-aunt, always so elegant, who — I learned at

her funeral — had hidden alone in a coal hole for 3

months. Or my father, 60 years an Englishman but

always feeling a foreigner. Inside him somewhere

the starving little boy hiding in a brick cellar in

Budapest, wearing his yellow star as nine-tenths

of his family died in the camps.

The Holocaust lived in my head. Teachers and friends told me I looked just like Anne Frank. Naturally, this added to my preoccupation. What would I do if they came back? And came for me? If they marched down the high street, kicking in the windows of the burger bar with their jackboots, glass shattering all over the pavement of my '80s childhood, where could I go? In our flat there was no attic; could I hide down in the cellar? If I dyed my hair blonde and tried to look less like Anne Frank could I pass?

I hatched daring escape plans.

My inheritance is the uninvited bad fairy who attended my birth, furious at her snub. Casting malevolent spells and evil shadows down through the generations. Her curse invades my thoughts without warning, she escapes the corners and makes incursions when I least expect it. In a steam room with friends, or smelling soaps in a beautiful shop. On a train through France. She will choose her moment to strike, flooding my body with a cold cortisol pulse and an urge to check all the exits. It is a hostile occupation.

In 2004 my Granny's hands wrote me a cheque for three thousand pounds. It was a ninth of the final restitution payments from the German government. She had been fighting for decades.

She said, as far as I am concerned it is blood money and I don't want it, so I've shared it out equally between you and your cousins. You must do something meaningful with it, do not fritter it away.

I paid for my master's degree, two years studying art in the evenings after work. Joy. It very much marked the start of a meaningful something. Those cheques helped my cousins to cars, trips, weddings. No one dared fritter.

The pleasure of the dark brown of the pub, settling in after a tutorial and chatting with new friends about the kind of art an old lady might hit with her cane.

But always lurking in the shadows beyond the wood panelling: that cigar box, those deadly debts. In fact, wherever I went and wherever I go

now, I see that the blood money paid for me to start to get to know her.

The studying, the art and the pub were the start of learning a language in which to talk about my inheritance.

Granny's life was amazing, though she would never have seen it that way. She ran through the 20th century without looking back. She was inappropriate and clever and gave out wet kisses and harsh uninvited opinions. She dropped hairpins everywhere: you could track her movements by the trail. She preferred Asda to Tesco and was ecstatic about her late-flowering love for Kofi Annan, then then UN secretary-general, whenever he came on the TV.

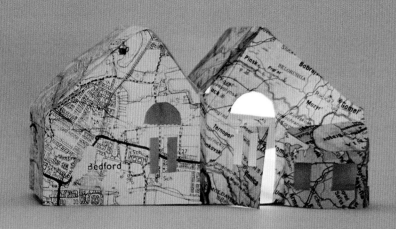

She lived in the same solid red-brick house for 50 years. She was always making something and would say often, (she was a terrible repeater) that she could not bear to have her hands still. I miss her and her busy hands and would love to be sat talking to her. Or at least listening. She tended to do all the talking.

One day in 2005 Granny drove me to Warrington Bank Quay station to get the train back to London. In my bag, a kilo of Lancashire cheese from Leigh market wrapped up in waxed paper. The air smelled of diesel and the sickly-sweet vapour from the Lever Brothers soap factory which towered towered over the station. She stood on the platform as the train started moving.

I waved from my side of the window; she waved back with both her hands, a blur of $9^2/_3$ fingers, getting smaller and smaller. She tracked my window for as long as she could, until the train was too fast and she lost me. I could just make her out as she stopped waving and turned, back bent, reaching for the handrail to go downstairs to the car park. Then she was gone.

Acknowledgements

First: Zadiks and adjacents. My brother and co-inheritor, Ben Gold. My cousins, Dan, Mike, Hannah, Sarah, Pete, Ruth and Mary, to whom she was also Granny, in great affection for all we share. Special thanks go to Ben, Dan and Mike, the cute knitwear models.

To Sue, Anthony, Paul, Sarah, Meg, and remembering Tom with much love. To the next generation: Emma, Sam, Mia, Oliver, Caleb, Phoebe, Lucy, Natalie and Cora and all of their parents.

I made this book on my day off each week from my job as a teacher, and am keenly aware how important our role is, though many would wrongly have it otherwise. I would not be writing these words if it weren't for the classes taught by Emily Haworth-Booth at the Royal Drawing School. Thank you, Emily.

I am grateful to the next wonderful teacher I had, Karrie Fransman and the LDComics mentoring programme. Without your encouragement, Karrie, I may not have told Elena's story.

I would like to thank the judges of the Emerging Writers Programme at the London Library 2022–23, especially Simon Garfield. Simon, your generosity and support proved invaluable; I am indebted to you.

Thanks and praise to Queen Claire Berliner and all who support the EWP. To my EWP peer support group: Melanie Carvalho, Melissa Richards, Carla Montemayor and Grahame Williams.

I am extremely fortunate to have Rosemary Scoular as my agent. Thank you, Rosemary, and all at United Agents, for your support and guidance: I have valued it so highly.

I would like to thank Hannah Westland for making a such welcoming home for this book. The process of refining the story with you was hugely enjoyable. Thanks also to everyone at Jonathan Cape.

Mensches, all of you.

To my beloved friends who looked after my kids so I could squeeze in a few more hours' work on a Saturday afternoon, who gave me late-night feedback, who sent sweary, excited texts from far and near, who asked me how the book was going, who encouraged and inspired me: you know who you are and I am so happy to be travelling along with you.

I would like to acknowledge the sheer brilliance of Polly Corrigan, whom I thought about every time I sat down to work, and all the days in between.

With great style, Eva gave excellent artistic and literary advice, for which I am very grateful. Thanks to Rosa for bringing gossip and making me smile every time she visited my desk, and for honest feedback whenever I bullied it out of her. Thank you to Natty for his infectious curiosity and hilarious one-liners. Jason I thank for his love, enthusiasm, support and all our many days. The word 'lucky' is just not enough. You four: my joy.

This book is dedicated to my parents, Tibor and Anne, in deep gratitude for everything, but especially for teaching me the priceless value of a book.

1 3 5 7 9 10 8 6 4 2

Jonathan Cape, an imprint of Vintage, is part of the
Penguin Random House group of companies whose addresses
can be found at global.penguinrandomhouse.com

First published by Jonathan Cape in 2024

'Miners' by Wilfred Owen from *The Penguin Book of First World
War Poetry*, first pub. 1979. Second edition pub. 1981.
With acknowledgement to the Wilfred Owen Literary Estate.

penguin.co.uk/vintage

Printed and bound in Dubai

The authorised representative in the EEA is Penguin Random House
Ireland, Morrison Chambers, 32 Nassau Street, Dublin D02 YH68

A CIP catalogue record for this book is available
from the British Library

ISBN 9781787335226